a guide to
stress relief

Sara Rose

p

This is a Parragon Book

This edition published in 2004

Parragon

Queen Street House

4 Queen Street

Bath BA1 1HE, UK

ISBN: 1-40542-592-X

Printed in China

Designed and created with

The Bridgewater Book Company Ltd.

NOTE

Any information given in this book is not intended to be
taken as a replacement for medical advice. Any person with
a condition requiring medical attention should consult
a qualified medical practitioner or therapist before
beginning this or any other exercise programme.

Contents

Introduction

The definition of good health is a sense of well-being. But all too often we become caught up in a cycle of stress and strain that leaves us functioning below our best and feeling tired, anxious and unhappy. This book offers practical advice to help overcome the pressures of modern life, maintain health and regain vitality and peace of mind.

For long-term stress relief and optimum well-being you need periods of mental and physical relaxation throughout the day. Relaxation is a set of easily learned skills that will teach you how to combat the effects of stress and restore the balance between body and mind to enable healthy, happy living.

This book shows simple but effective ways of making relaxation an integral part of your everyday life. This opening section describes the detrimental effects of too much strain on the body and mind. It will help you identify the

Many people practise meditation techniques to achieve inner calm and improve their sense of well-being.

traits that can undermine well-being so that you can make changes in your life for the better. Two chapters deal with physical and mental relaxation, and describe natural ways of restoring the balance between mind and body, using a variety of techniques taken from Eastern and Western traditions. The final chapter covers lifestyle factors and environmental influences.

Reconnecting with the natural world is a particularly effective way of alleviating the pressures of modern living. A spectacular sunset can both rejuvenate and refresh the senses.

Many physical, mental and emotional problems can be avoided if you put just a little effort into looking after yourself in a more caring way. This practical guide gives easy-to-follow advice for long-term calm and serenity, to help you unwind and enjoy life to the full.

Stress: the problem

The increasing demands of modern life put enormous pressure on the mind and body. Some stress is part of life and is not necessarily a bad thing: it is a normal response to danger, and positive stress provides the spur to achieve. But when stress is long-term it can affect you physically, emotionally and spiritually, impacting on your well-being.

Causes of stress

There is an enormous spectrum of 'stressors' (causes of stress) – from the relatively routine ring of the telephone to something life-threatening such as a car crash. Major life events, such as moving home, birth, marriage, divorce or death; environmental factors, such as noise, flashing lights, overcrowding, pollution; lifestyle, including poor diet and lack of sleep and exercise – these are just some of the things that can contribute to stress. Your own temperament, constitution and previous experiences moderate the effects of stress but the more stressors there are, the less you are able to deal with them effectively.

The stages of adaptation

Stress has very definite physical effects but it sometime takes years for you to notice this. In the 1950s an American doctor, Hans Selye, identified three stages of adaptation in the human response to long-term stress.

1. Alarm response

Exposure to stressors prompts an immediate biochemical reaction known as the 'fight or flight' response. Stress hormones are released into the bloodstream, causing the following:

- increased heart rate and blood pressure
- raised blood-sugar and cholesterol levels
- faster breathing and perspiration
- increased muscle tension
- disruption of digestive processes
- suppression of the immune system
- emotional tension

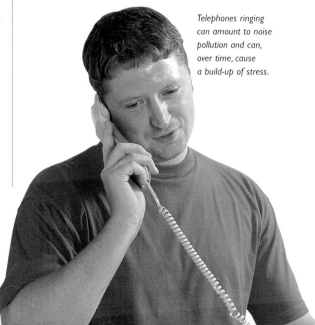

Telephones ringing can amount to noise pollution and can, over time, cause a build-up of stress.

2. Adaptation

If the cause of stress is removed or dealt with, the body reverts to normal functioning, but if it continues the body copes by adapting. Although you may feel as though everything has returned to normal, your body uses up energy stores and over time this affects your ability to function efficiently, resulting in fatigue, irritability and lethargy.

3. Exhaustion

Long-term stress changes the balance of hormones in the body and leads to exhaustion. A suppressed immune system, slower metabolism and slower rate of cell repair results in rapid ageing, weight gain and a greater risk of degenerative disease. Your body becomes run down, with recurring minor illnesses and psychological 'burn-out'. Eventually you may become seriously ill or suffer a breakdown.

But although stress may cause a variety of disorders, it is not in itself an illness. Stress is created by habitual responses to difficult situations and by an unhealthy lifestyle. It is a habit that you can break, if you are prepared to look carefully at your life and take control.

The body is an energy system that needs to keep balanced to function properly. Any kind of regular cardiovascular exercise – even walking – will keep the body in a healthy condition.

A balanced body

Your body's biochemical, structural and psychological functions are delicately balanced to enable good physical and mental health, and an upset in any one area can lead to problems in others. Optimum health requires looking after all parts of the whole. A healthy body and a clear and active mind with a positive attitude will help you maintain this balance.

A strategy for relaxation

The key to relaxation is to be able to recognise when you are under too much pressure and then dedicate time to looking after yourself. Developing the ability to relax at will during times of intense pressure, as well as implementing long-term strategies for dealing with stress, will help you feel calmer and more in control of your life.

Benefits of relaxation

Relaxation can counter many of the effects of stress. Adrenaline levels decrease, reducing stress on the cardiovascular system and lowering blood pressure. Breathing becomes slower and more controlled. The muscles become less tense and digestive processes improve. The immune system becomes more active, making you less susceptible to illness.

Insomnia, coupled with constant tiredness, may be a sign that your immune system is under strain and that you need to change something in your life.

Recognising stress

The symptoms of stress generally manifest in behavioural, emotional and physical ways. If you regularly experience more than five of the following, you need to take action.

Behavioural:

- excessive drinking or smoking

- poor appetite or overeating

- avoiding others and an inability to enjoy company

Emotional:

- irritability, anger and readiness to explode for no apparent reason

- difficulties in decision-making, concentration or memory

- feelings of being overwhelmed and unable to cope

   - depression

   - tearfulness

   - no sense of humour

Back or neck ache are two of the many ways that stress manifests itself.

Physical:

* constant tiredness

* insomnia

* clumsiness

* muscular aches and pains including backache and headaches

* skin problems

* high blood pressure

* palpitations and panic attacks

* breathing problems including asthma, shallow breathing and hyperventilation

* indigestion, heartburn, ulcers, nervous diarrhoea or constipation

You can't always avoid stress but being able to identify what causes it is the first step towards helping yourself cope better. In some cases you can take active steps to lead a calmer life – for example, if you find shopping stressful, why not order your groceries online instead?

Relaxation

Learn how to relax during times of great stress. Think of an activity that you associate with being calm, such as lying in the sun or having a warm bath. When you feel under pressure, think about your relaxation activity. Your mind will associate this with peace and you will soon start to feel relaxed.

On the record

Although you may recognise the symptoms of stress, it is sometimes difficult to pinpoint the cause. Keeping a record will help you to identify patterns of stress in your life.

1

Divide each page into sections, either an hourly breakdown, or for different times of the day (eg breakfast, morning, lunchtime, afternoon, evening).

2

Make a note of all your activities during the day and how you were feeling at the time.

3

Fill in your diary whenever a stress symptom occurs. If possible, make a note of what happened just before it occurred.

4

At the end of the week, evaluate the times when you felt stressed and when you felt relaxed.

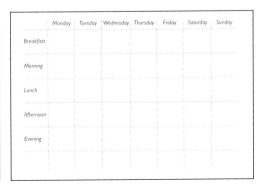

	Monday	Tuesday	Wednesday	Thursday	Friday	Saturday	Sunday
Breakfast							
Morning							
Lunch							
Afternoon							
Evening							

PART I: RELAXING YOUR BODY

Introduction

Efficient, controlled breathing and the ability to relax at will are vital in dealing effectively with stress. Simple breathing exercises and muscle relaxation techniques reduce the mental and physical effects of stress and enhance well-being. Touch and movement therapies benefit mind and body by increasing energy levels and engendering a sense of deep relaxation.

You can practise many different techniques originating from all over the world to enhance physical relaxation. You do not need to perform them all as part of your daily routine, but it is worth at least trying out as many as possible so that you can discover which are the most beneficial and comfortable for you. Some of these techniques normally depend on having a willing partner with you, but you can still reap the benefits of massage or reflexology by yourself.

Once you have found a range of relaxing exercises that suit you, it is important to develop a regular routine in the same way you would with any sport or exercise discipline. To see the true benefits you need to make it a part of your lifestyle rather than something that you do as a break from your routine. The small amount of time spent relaxing your body muscles and controlling your breathing each morning or evening will pay dividends over the rest of the day. Some people may find it more convenient to perform relaxing exercises in the evening, helping them unwind and preparing them for sleep. Should you do so, however, remember not to do any form of physical exercise straight after a meal or in the hours before going to bed.

Relaxed, controlled breathing exercises before you go to work in the morning will put you in the right mood for a successful day.

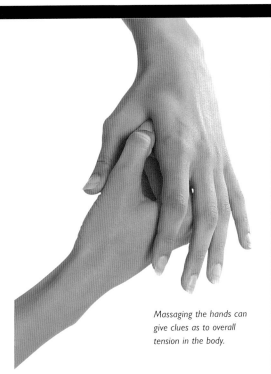

Massaging the hands can give clues as to overall tension in the body.

A space to relax

Just like any other form of physical exercise, your environment and clothing are as important as the routine you undertake. If at all possible, find a comfortable room that is without distractions – it will be far more difficult to relax if the television is on in the corner of the room. You should also be wearing loose-fitting clothing that allows you to move and breathe freely.

Although you should find that following a regular routine will provide you with a greater capacity to deal with stress in your day-to-day living, you will undoubtedly still be faced with unexpected crises at work or home. At such times you may find that taking a break to spend a few minutes working on your breathing or massaging yourself can put you in the right frame of mind to concentrate on finding a

positive solution to the problem and so avoid being overwhelmed by the problem itself. Whichever routine you choose, it should improve your health and sense of well-being and help you deal with life's challenges more easily and with less stress.

This yoga position, a reversed Namaste (Prayer pose) is good for stretching the shoulders and arm muscles and expanding the chest.

Breathing

Correct breathing is the key to calming mind and body. How you breathe reflects your health and how you feel about yourself. Your breathing becomes shallow and rapid when you are anxious, but slow and deep when you are at ease. Years of stress and poor lifestyle means that rapid, shallow breathing is the norm for most of us.

Breathing is essential to life. As you breathe, oxygen is taken into the bloodstream and fuels the production of energy that enables your body to function. Breathing is an automatic, involuntary activity, but it can be consciously controlled. In times of acute stress, taking a minute to slow down and control your breathing will calm you instantly.

Correct, effective breathing should come from the deepest area of the lungs.

The effects of poor breathing

When stress levels rise, breathing tends to use only the top third of the lungs. There is a drop in levels of carbon dioxide, which is needed to maintain blood acidity, and harmful toxins are not breathed out. This has a direct detrimental effect on the nerves and muscles, and may result in tiredness, palpitations and panic attacks. If you learn to breathe properly, these conditions can be alleviated and you will also benefit from a lower heart-rate, reduced blood pressure and lower levels of stress hormones. So there are many benefits of learning to breathe correctly.

Breathing for health

Deeper breathing and a slower pulse are recognised signs of good health – the deeper the breath, the more body tissues can be oxygenated, and the stronger your heart is, the less often it needs to beat.

How to breathe

To improve your breathing you must first become aware of it. If you find your breathing is too fast or too shallow, the following exercise – known as abdominal breathing – will help you breathe more naturally. It uses the diaphragm (the sheet of muscle forming the top of the abdomen) to enable the lungs to inflate and deflate with minimal effort.

1

Sit in a comfortable position with your eyes open or closed. Place one hand on your chest and the other over your diaphragm just below the breastbone. Breathe in slowly through your nose, and try to breathe so that the hand on your chest remains relatively still.

2

Hold your breath for a few seconds then breathe out slowly through your nose. Release as much air as possible.

3

Repeat for a few minutes until you feel calm.

Alternate nostril breathing

Blow your nose to clear the nasal passages. Place your forefinger and second finger on your forehead, with the thumb and third finger on either side of your nose. Relax your thumb and inhale through that nostril then close with the thumb. Release your third finger and exhale through the other nostril. Continue to breathe in and out through alternate nostrils. This exercise helps you become aware of each breath, but stop if you feel dizzy.

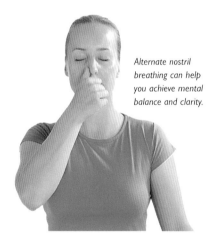

Alternate nostril breathing can help you achieve mental balance and clarity.

Life force

Many Eastern philosophies believe that as well as containing oxygen, air also contains vital energy (known as *prana* in India, *qi* or *chi* in China and *ki* in Japan). By performing conscious breathing exercises you can accumulate this energy and revitalise both your mind and your body.

Reducing muscle tension

When your body and mind are under pressure, your muscles become constricted. Tight, cramped muscles restrict the body's blood supply, causing pain, fatigue and tension. Over-tense muscles can dramatically affect your posture, movement, and body functioning. To relax, you must first locate the tension and try to release it.

Progressive muscle relaxation

This relaxation technique, which tenses and releases all the major muscle groups, will help you to slow down and let go of muscle tension. Choose a quiet time of day when you will not be disturbed.

1

Remove your shoes and loosen tight clothing. Lie on a mat on the floor or a firm bed, with a pillow under your head for support. Close your eyes and focus on breathing slowly, emphasising the out-breath.

2

Tense the muscles in your right foot, hold for a few seconds then release. Tense and release the calf, then the thigh muscles. Repeat with the left foot and leg.

3

Tense and release the muscles in your right hand and arm, then the left.

4

Tense and release each buttock, then the stomach muscles.

5

Lift your shoulders up to your ears, hold for a few seconds, then lower. Repeat three times. Rock your head gently from side to side.

6

Yawn, then pout. Frown, wrinkle your nose and let go. Raise your eyebrows then relax your face muscles.

7

Focus on your breathing again. Wriggle your fingers and toes, bend your knees and gently roll on to your side, then get up slowly.

Alexander technique

This method of self-awareness, devised by an Australian actor, aims to improve balance, posture and coordination so that the body can operate with minimum strain. By learning to stand and move correctly, you can alleviate muscular tension and enable the body systems to function more efficiently.

The technique consists of three stages: releasing unwanted tension; learning new ways of moving, standing or sitting; and learning new ways of reacting physically and mentally to various situations. It should be learned from a qualified teacher and practised regularly.

Flotation and water therapy

Flotation tanks are sound-proofed tanks of warm water in which salts and minerals have been dissolved to enable the body to float effortlessly. This is a way of isolating body and mind from external stimuli in order to induce deep relaxation. During flotation the body and mind become profoundly relaxed and the brain releases endorphins, natural painkillers.

Hot water dilates blood vessels, reducing blood pressure. For a simple home remedy to relax stiff muscles, soak in a warm bath.

Massage

Using touch is a very effective way of becoming relaxed, and massage is one of the easiest and most reliable ways of relieving stress and relaxing painful muscles. This soothing therapy releases tension and reduces anxiety. There are numerous kinds of massage, many of which have been incorporated into various complementary therapies.

Physical effects of massage

Gentle massage stimulates sensory nerve endings in the skin, which transmit messages through the nervous system to the brain. The brain responds by releasing endorphins, natural painkillers that induce a feeling of well-being. Massage further aids relaxation by affecting the body systems that control blood pressure, heart rate, digestion and breathing, resulting in increased health.

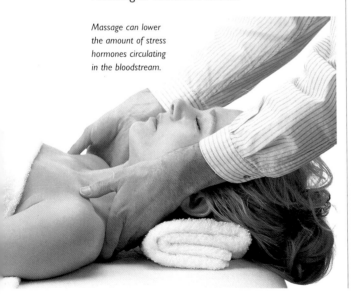

Massage can lower the amount of stress hormones circulating in the bloodstream.

Neck and shoulder massage

Tense, aching muscles are usually felt in the neck and shoulders. When you are tired, your posture tends to slump, straining your neck and shoulder muscles. It is extremely relaxing to have someone massage your neck and shoulders, but you can easily massage yourself.

Receiving massage

Make sure the room is warm and comfortable, then undress and lie down. Your partner should warm his or her hands then place a few drops of massage oil into the palms and knead the skin around your shoulder blades for a few minutes. Your partner can then place his or her hands between the tops of the shoulder blades and rotate the thumbs to massage lightly down the sides of the spine (not pressing on the bones) and along the shoulder blades. Your partner can finish the massage by squeezing the shoulder muscles to release deep-seated tension.

Self-massage

Shrug your shoulders and push them back as far as possible. Hold for five seconds then release. Repeat five times. Put your hand at the top of your arm and knead the flesh firmly, moving slowly towards your neck. Repeat three times. Press your fingers into the back of your neck and move the fingertips in a circular motion towards the base of the skull. Repeat five times. Holding the back of your head, rotate your thumbs at the base of your skull.

Quick fixes for headaches

Smooth the tips of your fingers over your forehead, working from the centre to the temples. Now place your palm on your forehead with your fingers pointing horizontally and gently move it up towards your hairline. Repeat with the other hand and continue until the tension ebbs away.

Regular hand massage can help relieve joint problems and arthritis.

Hand massage

Massage the web between your thumb and forefinger, using the opposite hand to press as close as possible to the point where the two bones meet. Continue for about a minute then repeat on the other hand. This is a technique employed in acupressure, an ancient Chinese form of massage and healing.

Caution

Do not massage swellings, fractures, bruises or infected skin. The stomach, legs and feet should not be massaged in the first trimester of pregnancy. If you suffer from varicose veins, back pain or thrombosis, seek professional medical advice before having any massage treatment.

Restoring vital energy

Every day we accumulate stress, which is stored in our minds as anxiety and in our bodies as tension. Many philosophies hold that tension blocks the flow of vital energy and prevents us from being rejuvenated. Therapies that unblock this tension have been devised to restore your body's state of equilibrium.

Yoga

Yoga has been practised in India for thousands of years and is now popular around the world. There are many types of yoga but the form most common in the West is 'hatha' yoga, which means balance of mind and body. This comprises body postures (*asanas*) and breathing techniques (*pranayama*) to prepare the body so that the mind can meditate without obstructions or obstacles.

Breathing correctly is the key to hatha yoga, and when done properly every movement is coordinated with the breath. Each *asana* is designed to stretch and strengthen the body, and is generally held for between 20 seconds and two minutes.

Everyone can practise yoga, regardless of fitness or age, but when learning it is advisable to attend classes held by a qualified teacher. Regular daily practice will increase energy and stamina, tone muscles, improve digestion and concentration, and help you relax and deal with life's daily stresses.

Natarajasana, *or the Dancer position, helps strengthen the muscles in the legs, feet and lower back, as well as improving balance.*

Precautions

If you suffer from back pain, high blood pressure, or heart disease, or if you are pregnant, consult your doctor before starting a new exercise regime. When practising yoga, certain postures such as headstands should be avoided during pregnancy or menstruation and others are not suitable if you have certain medical conditions – consult your yoga teacher first.

The physical benefits of the ancient Chinese practice of T'ai Chi *include toned and strengthened muscles, more efficient internal organs, improved posture and increased circulation.*

T'ai Chi

This ancient Chinese martial art uses sequences of slow, graceful movements and breathing techniques to relax mind and body. *T'ai Chi* exercises aim to restore the balance of *qi* and enhance health and vitality.

Flow of *qi*

Ancient Chinese philosophy teaches the concept of *yin* and *yang*, opposite but complementary forces whose balance within the body is essential for well-being. The interaction of *yin* and *yang* gives rise to *qi* or *chi*, an invisible 'life force' that flows around the body. The free circulation of *qi* is vital for good health: illness is thought to be caused by a blockage of *qi*.

Reflexology

Foot and hand massage have long been used to promote relaxation and improve health. The hands and feet are considered to be a mirror of the body and pressure on specific reflex points is thought to affect corresponding body parts. Reflexologists believe that granular deposits accumulate around reflex points, blocking energy flow, and the aim is to break down these deposits and improve the blood supply to flush away toxins.

Reflexology is generally performed on the feet by a trained practitioner and is deeply relaxing, but you can easily massage your hands at any time to relieve stress.

When pain, discomfort or illness is found somewhere in the body, a good reflexologist can use reflexology maps of the feet to discover which part of the foot should be treated.

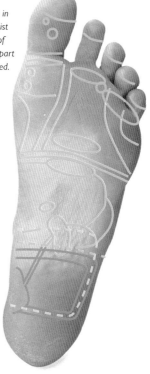

PART 2: RELAXING MIND AND SPIRIT

Introduction

Your thoughts, moods, emotions and beliefs have a fundamental impact on your basic health, healing mechanisms and immune system. To be truly healthy you need to look after your mind as well as your body. There are many different types of mind therapies designed for mental relaxation and to reverse the stress response. To a certain extent the type of person you are will determine how you react to a stressful event, but there are techniques you can learn to improve your self-image that will give you the ability to cope better with life's many challenges and difficulties.

The techniques described in this section, such as meditation and visualisation, offer ways of relaxing your mind so that you can control its responses to stress, and also enable you to change the way you think about yourself and the challenges that you face.

Focus your senses on a favourite piece of music to find inner calm.

Know your mind

Relaxing your mind is the natural complement to relaxing your body, and to be able to deal with stress you need to master your ability to do both. For those who are not used to meditating and other forms of controlling their thoughts it may not feel natural at first but, as with any form of exercise, regular practice will soon lead to it becoming second nature.

Mental relaxation, like physical relaxation, requires a calm and comfortable environment to be effective, and you will find it far easier to separate your mind from your immediate surroundings if your senses are not being bombarded by the bustle of life around you. Indeed, in both meditation and visualisation, many people find it easier if they have something relaxing to focus their senses on, whether it is peaceful music, images of a beautiful, calming scene or a favourite aroma. These need not be physically present – even the memories of such sensations can help you to relax and take control of your mind.

As you become more experienced in controlling your mind's reactions, however, you may find that you are able to switch to a relaxed state despite the distractions around you, a situation that has obvious benefits for dealing with stressful situations.

Along with the need to relax your mind and control its responses to stress, the need to change the way you think about yourself and your life is important. Few people realise the destructive impact on their lives of thinking about what they haven't achieved, the unattainable goals they set themselves or even negative things that have not yet occurred. Learning to think about what you have achieved and setting realistic goals is a valuable way of avoiding generating unnecessary stress.

Mental relaxation is not based on purely internal factors, however, and relationships with other people can provide happiness and calm in your daily life and support in the most difficult of times. Developing and strengthening your relationships with family and friends is also vital to achieving inner calm.

Visualising a favourite place can help you achieve a positive frame of mind in the most trying of times.

Meditation

Meditation is an effective way of focusing your mind to bring about relaxation, peace and tranquillity. It will help you to gain a new perspective and enable you to stand back from your problems. Meditation is often practised as a means of spiritual self-enlightenment, but it can also be used to relieve stress and promote relaxation.

What is meditation?

There are various types of meditation but they all focus on quietening the mind. The intention is to direct your concentration so that it is filled with peace and calm and cannot take off on its own and become stressed. When the mind is calm and focused in the present it is neither reacting to memories nor worrying over the future, two major sources of chronic stress. Meditation techniques can be divided into two basic groups:

Meditation is a practical and effective way of dealing with stress.

1. Concentrative meditation

This focuses your attention on something specific, such as the intake of breath, or an image or a phrase, in order to still the mind and facilitate the emergence of a greater awareness and clarity.

2. 'Mindfulness' meditation

Also known as *vipassana*, or 'passive awareness', this describes a state of mind where you are aware of, but detached from, everything you are experiencing. Your attention is aware of sensations, feelings, images, thoughts and sounds without thinking about them; you observe without making judgements. This means experiencing what happens in the here and now to gain a calmer, clearer and non-reactive state of mind. If you use the analogy of a camera, it is like looking through a wide-angle lens – you experience more and your attention becomes broader.

Meditation and the brain

The brain is the body's computer, the centre of all our thoughts, feelings and sensory experiences, and the coordinator of all our bodily functions. The brain sends and receives messages via the spinal cord to all parts of the body. Brain cells communicate with each other by producing tiny electrical impulses. Meditation affects the electrical activity of the brain, causing the production of high-intensity alpha waves – brain waves associated with deep relaxation and mental alertness. These in turn help to undermine our habitual stressed responses to dangers and difficulties.

During alpha-wave states the part of the nervous system that governs automatic body functions – such as breathing, perspiration, salivation, digestion and heart rate – predominates, reversing the 'fight-or-flight' response to danger and stress.

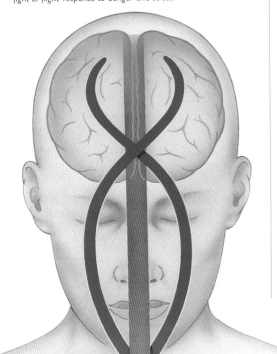

The brain produces four types of brain waves, which indicate our physical state: alpha (when we are deeply relaxed), beta (awake), delta (during a state of deep sleep) and theta (light sleep).

The benefits of meditation

Being able to control your mind instead of allowing your mind to control you will bring peace and harmony into your life. Those who meditate regularly are less anxious, calmer, mentally more alert and more efficient in managing time and energy. Research suggests that meditation confers the following benefits:

* more relaxed body

* improved sleeping patterns

* lower blood pressure and reduced pulse rate

* lower levels of stress hormones in the blood

* improved circulation

How to meditate

It helps to consult a teacher who can show you how to achieve a meditative state but you can teach yourself if you are sufficiently disciplined. There is no 'right' way to meditate but in order to do so successfully there are a few basic requirements to follow.

- a quiet place where you will not be disturbed

- regular practice, preferably for 15 minutes a day at the same time of day – meditation in the morning helps you to feel calm and centred for the rest of the day; meditation at night allows you to wind down

- an empty stomach

- a comfortable position (usually sitting to stop you from falling asleep)

- a focus for the mind to help you withdraw from your environment

Household items, such as a plant, candle or picture, can provide a focus for object-centred meditation.

Focusing the mind

You may find it difficult to concentrate at first, but this will improve with practice. You may also feel sleepy to begin with but as you meditate for longer you will feel more alert. If you feel your attention wandering, just bring it back to the focus of meditation. People usually achieve a meditative state by one of the following methods:

Using an object such as a flower for meditation can help keep the mind concentrated and attention focused.

Object meditation

Concentrate on a particular object, feeling its presence and focusing on its texture, shape and other qualities. A crystal, a candle flame, a flower or a mandala (a picture with a focal point) are all suitable objects.

Chanting a mantra or phrase, such as the sacred 'om', can help you maintain concentration and meditate successfully.

Mantra meditation

A 'mantra' is a word or phrase repeated continually, either silently or aloud. The Hindu 'aum' or 'om' is a sacred mantra that is widely used, though any word could be suitable.

Touch

Rhythmically passing a rosary or worry beads through the fingers, or rubbing a piece of fabric, can induce a state of meditation.

Breath awareness

Focus on your breathing to achieve a state of meditation. Count 'one' on each out-breath.

Active meditation

Rhythmic exercise such as *T'ai Chi*, swimming or walking can focus the mind and are more energising than sitting still.

Exercise: Quick and easy meditation

1

Sit comfortably with your spine straight. Look downwards, but not focusing on anything.

2

Let your eyelids drop to a level that feels comfortable without closing your eyes completely.

3

Continue to look downwards. You should notice that your breathing is slower and deeper.

4

Return your eyes to their normal focus after a couple of minutes. You should feel relaxed and calm.

Caution

Consult your doctor before starting meditation if you have a history of psychiatric disorders. Long-term meditation sometimes causes depression and withdrawal.

Visualisation

Visualisation, a technique that harnesses the imagination to deal with stress and illness, improve motivation and change negative attitudes, is an important part of many relaxation therapies, and is used by athletes. Through imagining sights, sounds, tastes or smells, you can use positive thinking to restore and maintain good health.

Self-help

Although you can consult a professional teacher to learn visualisation, it is possible to learn the technique on your own. At first, you will probably need to practise for 15–20 minutes a day, either first thing in the morning or last thing at night, but as you become more skilled you should be able to do it for just a few minutes at a time as needed.

Choose a quiet, comfortable place where you won't be disturbed. Breathe slowly and try to relax your body. Then focus on your chosen image. It helps to repeat positive affirmations as you do this, such as 'I feel relaxed' or 'I am in control'. You can perform this exercise in times of stress and it will help you gain control of a difficult or challenging situation.

Now visualise a calm, beautiful scene, real or imaginary, to help you relax. Suitable images include a peaceful garden, a beach, or a room. Try to envisage the sounds, smells and sights of the scene and soak up the atmosphere until you feel truly relaxed.

Visualising a calm, serene scene, such as a deserted sandy beach, is an effective way of using the imagination to help you relax and overcome stress and anxiety.

Fear of situations

Most people experience some degree of nerves or panic before important occasions, but visualisation can help you feel more in control. For example, for several days before the event, anticipate dealing successfully with a job interview, or imagine the round of applause after public speaking, and the affirmation will take root in your subconscious.

Imagery can also be used to overcome stress. Think of an image that you associate with tension (such as a thunderstorm) and replace it with something calming (a rainbow).

Powerful, tense scenes – such as a thunderstorm – can be imagined and replaced with something calming, like a rainbow, to help induce inner calm.

Colour visualisation

Colour can have a profound effect on your mood, vitality and well-being. Yellows and reds are stimulating: blues and greens calming. Colour therapists use different colours to improve your physical, emotional and spiritual health, generally by shining coloured lights onto your body. This exercise uses colour visualisation to calm the mind and help you relax.

1

Sit comfortably with your eyes closed.

2

Imagine a ball of golden light just above your head. Visualise the ball of light slowly descending through your head until it fills your entire body. Imagine that this light is cleansing and healing your spirit.

3

Repeat, visualising a ball of red light. Continue slowly through the colour spectrum – orange, yellow, green, blue, indigo and violet – until you feel completely relaxed.

The sound of crashing waves can be soothing, helping you to relieve stress and create inner calm.

Music and sounds

The therapeutic potential of music and sounds has long been recognised. Sound waves vibrate at different frequencies and have emotional and physical results, affecting your moods, heart rate, breathing and even prompting the release of endorphins. Whether or not you can sing in tune, the very act of singing releases tension and encourages you to breathe deeply and rhythmically. Making or responding to music can connect you directly to your inner self, enabling you to express profound emotions. Soft, quiet music will calm you down, while loud music stirs the soul.

A relaxation tape

Making your own relaxation tape is much more effective than buying one off the shelf. Choose a gentle, relaxing piece of music, lasting for at least 10 minutes, that you associate with pleasant memories. Add some sounds of nature if you like (for example, birdsong, a breeze rustling through the trees, or sounds of the sea).

Choose a quiet room to relax in, sit or lie down, close your eyes and play the tape. Try to match the rhythm of your breathing to that of the music, and conjure up pleasant mental images as you do so. Listen to the tape once a day if possible, and soon you will be able to use the memory of this music to calm you down in times of stress.

Release healing endorphins by listening to your favourite music or sounds from nature.

Therapeutic touch

One of the surest ways of soothing stress is through touch. However, physical contact does not have to be sexual. Stroking a cat or giving someone a hug can be just as effective. For a quick relief from stress, sit quietly for a moment with your index finger touching the thumb of the same hand. Massage is another tried and tested way of relaxing and alleviating stress (see pages 16–17).

Sense of smell

Different aromas can lift your mood and make you feel much better about yourself. Smell molecules travel along the olfactory pathways and directly into the limbic system, which is the part of the brain that controls memories, instincts and vital functions. For this reason, some smells are intensely evocative and can conjure up vivid scenes from nearly forgotten memories. Fragrant aromatherapy oils are used in a number of ways to aid relaxation (see pages 58–59).

You can also use the memory of scent and its powers of association to help you stay calm and relaxed during times of stress. Think about your favourite smells – a baby's skin, freshly ground coffee, oranges, the smell of frying bacon, your favourite flowers, new-mown grass – and you will instantly feel happier, more carefree and more relaxed.

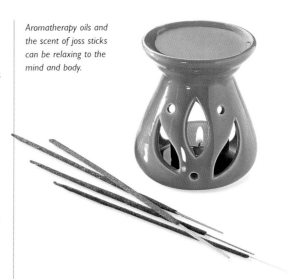

Aromatherapy oils and the scent of joss sticks can be relaxing to the mind and body.

Creative relaxation

Creative activities such as painting, drawing and sculpting are excellent outlets for your emotions and can be deeply relaxing. Talent is not an issue – you do not need to produce a 'good' work of art. The mere act of performing an activity that is creative rather than a chore is relaxing in itself. Let yourself become aware of the different textures and aromas of the art media you are using – whether paints, crayons, chalks or clay – and enjoy the experience.

Visiting an art gallery can also be relaxing, particularly if you find a favourite picture or painting that has special associations for you. Go during a quiet time of day when you can sit and contemplate a piece without being disturbed.

More techniques for mind control

There are several other mind techniques you can be taught to reverse the body's stress response, including hypnotherapy, autogenic training and biofeedback. All these will help you relax and take control of your life.

Hypnotherapy

A hypnotic trance is a state of consciousness similar to daydreaming, which can be used to change patterns of behaviour and promote positive thinking. While you are in a hypnotic state you are very relaxed and open to suggestions. One theory to explain this is that under hypnosis the conscious, rational part of the brain is bypassed (the left hemisphere) and the subconscious, non-analytical part (the right hemisphere) takes over. During hypnosis the practitioner may 'feed' suggestions to your subconscious mind to overcome a specific problem, such as nicotine addiction or lack of confidence; or he or she might ask about past experiences to analyse current problems. A hypnotherapist can take you into a state of deep relaxation, which you may be able to recreate when faced with stressful situations.

Self-hypnosis

Most people can learn to hypnotise themselves. Find a place where you are unlikely to be disturbed and sit quietly or lie down. Relax and breathe slowly and deeply. Close your eyes and imagine yourself walking down a country lane, or descending a staircase, counting down from ten to zero as you go. Repeat positive affirmations to deal with your problem, or listen to a prerecorded tape of yourself. Bring yourself out of hypnosis by reversing the method with which you entered the hypnotic state.

To fully relax and go into a state of hypnosis, the mind has to envisage a quiet place, such as a country lane or a tranquil sky.

Caution

Hypnotherapy and autogenic training can be harmful to those who suffer from disorders such as severe depression, psychosis or epilepsy. Always consult a qualified and reputable practitioner.

Autogenic training

Autogenic means 'generated from within' and describes the way in which your mind can influence your body to train your autonomic nervous system – the part of the brain that governs automatic body functions – to become relaxed. Autogenic training (AT) consists of six silent mental exercises that enable you to switch off the body's stress response at will. With practice you should reach an altered state of consciousness known as 'passive concentration', a state of awareness similar to meditation whereby you relax by not actively working to do so.

Autogenic training seems to work best when performed in a sequence and with set phrases, such as 'my right arm is heavy, my left arm is heavy, both of my arms are heavy'. Each exercise is designed to relax different areas of the body. Once learned, the technique can be practised at home. AT needs to be performed on a regular basis to maintain the technique and ensure its continued effectiveness.

When in a state of hypnosis, the mind is very relaxed and open to suggestions, offering hypnotherapists the opportunity to replace negative thoughts and associations with positive ones.

Biofeedback

Biofeedback is a way of monitoring and controlling unconscious biological functions through electronic devices. It can also help you monitor your response to stress. Probes or electrodes are attached to your body and connected to electronic 'biofeedback' instruments that monitor physical responses. While getting feedback you perform relaxation exercises to regulate body functions until you reach a state of relaxation.

A sense of self

How you feel about yourself is key to becoming relaxed and overcoming stress. Anything you can do to sustain a more positive frame of mind will be beneficial to your physical health. You need to be confident about who you are and what you want to achieve – this will help you successfully manage your life and your relationships.

Improving self-worth

It is all too easy to belittle your own abilities and achievements, and most of us regularly make negative statements about ourselves without even realising it. But if you value yourself and your positive attributes, other people will value you as well.

Pioneered in the 1920s by French pharmacist Emile Coué, autosuggestion is a simple but effective technique that can change the way you think about yourself and the way you react to others. It consists of repeating simple, positive statements, made in the present tense, such as 'Every day, in every way, I am getting better and better'. Autosuggestion is most effective when you use preplanned and memorised phrases as a part of meditation or visualisation.

Improve your self-worth by affirming your good characteristics and repeating positive statements to yourself.

Set yourself attainable life goals – write a plan or a series of steps to move toward them.

Setting goals

Change is inevitable and desirable, but can be deeply unnerving as it pushes us out into the unknown. When contemplating long-term, positive change, it will help you on your way to identify some short-term, attainable goals. First you need to think of goals you would like to achieve in different areas of your life – relationships, work, money matters, healthy lifestyle, for example – within a specific time frame; but these need to be realistic, and don't try to change too much at once. Write them down and think of at least three steps you can take to reach each one. Reward yourself after each step on the way. If a particular goal seems unattainable, perhaps you need to give yourself more steps to reach it, or maybe you are simply being unrealistic and need to modify what you are trying to achieve.

Going with the flow

In order to stay relaxed you have to accept that you only have control over your own actions. Fighting to control the world around you is exhausting and often unsuccessful. But if you accept that life is full of obstacles, they become easier to deal with.

Laughing it off

As well as being fun, laughing gives the heart and lungs a good workout, and research indicates that it also lowers blood pressure, relaxes muscles, reduces pain, reduces stress hormones, and boosts the immune system by increasing the production of disease-destroying cells. Laughter triggers the release of endorphins, the body's natural painkiller, and produces a general sense of well-being.

Living for the moment

Small children have a wonderful facility for enjoying the moment, because they are free of the heavy burden of the past and have not yet learned to fear the future. As adults we are so conditioned to think of a hundred things at once that we often find it difficult to break free and just 'be' in the here and now. Many Eastern philosophies incorporate the idea of 'mindfulness' – being acutely aware of the present by keeping the mind fully absorbed in the task you are performing.

Mindfulness is a technique that can be learned, although it takes practice to stop your attention from wandering. Next time you have to perform an unwelcome task (such as doing the ironing), instead of daydreaming, concentrate fully on the job in hand. Focus on the rhythmic movement of your chore. When you become fully involved in the moment, even the most mundane tasks can focus your mind, helping you to feel calm and centred.

Performing everyday tasks, such as washing up the dishes, can help you achieve mindfulness. Concentrate fully on the job in hand.

Positive commuting

Negative feelings sap your energy and set up a self-perpetuating cycle of disappointment, worry and regret. Positive thinking gives you hope, and once set into motion you will feel better about many aspects of your life.

With practice you can change negative thoughts into positive ones. Think of an activity you find stressful – for example, commuting to work each day. Start by focusing on the downside (the wasted time, or the tiredness induced by a long journey). Tell these thoughts to go away. Consciously switch your negative thoughts to positive ones – think of using the time spent commuting to read, meditate or listen to music.

With practice, it can become second nature to think of the positive things in life, rather than the negative.

Count your blessings

Competition and striving for material success causes much of the stress in our society, and it is all too easy to forget the truly important things in life. Take a few moments each day to think carefully about the good things you have. These can be anything – good relationships, special skills, good health or happy children. Forget about competing for more things and feel at peace with yourself.

Freedom from fear

No one can be absolutely certain what lies ahead and often fear of what the future may hold prevents our enjoyment of the present. Instead of thinking about the what ifs? (what if I lose my job/become ill/can't pay my mortgage, for example), stop worrying and enjoy what you have at the moment. Visualisation exercises, which enable you to create an image of the future as you want it to be, are particularly beneficial in helping you to look forward to the future, rather than dreading it, but again this should be something achievable and not just a fantasy. You may find it helps to dedicate a certain time of day for thinking about your worries. When the time is up, just stop thinking about them.

Relationships

Maintaining good relationships with family and friends gives you emotional support and makes you feel more positive, thus reducing stress levels and engendering calm. All relationships need to be worked at, so that everyone feels valued and loved.

Improving your relationships

Learn to listen to what others have to say and in return they will respond to you. Practise kindness, tolerance, forgiveness and trust. Confide in your friends or family, and tell them how you are feeling.

Friends

For many people in the Western world, it is friends rather than family who provide emotional support, and just as we sometimes do with family members, we often take friends for granted. It is important to make time to show your appreciation for your friends, and to reflect upon the benefits they bring.

Partners

Successful adult partnerships provide support, security and fulfilment, and physical and emotional communication is essential for a stress-free relationship. To make the most of your partnership it is vital to take time to be with each other. To promote intimacy in your relationship, try the following:

- Establish the mood by lighting candles and playing soft, relaxing music.

- Add aphrodisiac essential oils such as ylang ylang or jasmine to a massage oil, and give each other a sensual, soothing massage.

- Add essential oils to a warm bath, or burn in a vaporiser in the bedroom to give it a sensual scent.

- Take a relaxing bath together.

- Talk about the good things in your life, and plans for the future.

When spending time with your partner, burning aromatic candles can be a perfect way to create an intimate atmosphere.

Take time to enjoy your children; play with them, and their enthusiasm and vitality will rub off on you.

Discussion

Relationships are much more open and fulfiling if you are honest with each other about your problems and needs. But you still need to maintain a degree of tact and try to avoid hurtful statements and actions.

- Set aside a time for discussion, but reschedule if either of you is tired, stressed or has had too much to drink.

- Think carefully about what you want to say beforehand – jot down a list of points you want to discuss.

- Try to be positive rather than focusing on the negative aspects of a situation.

- Don't hold your discussions in the bedroom, especially just before you are going to sleep, and avoid using a room where you would usually relax – you may even prefer to go for a walk, away from the home.

- Once you have reached an agreed conclusion, reaffirm your love for each other.

Children

Children are physically, emotionally and financially draining. However, they are also an endless source of pleasure and unconditional love, and they grow up all too quickly.

Bereavement

The death of a loved one is a source of profound stress. Grief increases your susceptibility to illness and diminishes your ability to cope. Grieving is a process that passes through various stages, including shock, denial, anger and finally acceptance. Expressing your emotions will prevent you from becoming overwhelmed by grief.

When grieving, don't bottle up your emotions – this will only prolong the pain and could lead to mental health problems.

Introduction

Just a few simple adjustments to your lifestyle and environment can reap untold benefits for your general health and vitality. Making these changes is part of the process of taking more care of yourself. By organising your work and leisure more effectively, you will feel on top of your problems and in control of your life.

While relaxing our minds teaches us to appreciate the present and not to worry unduly about the future, it does not mean that we should not think about the day ahead of us. It is common not to take stock of how we live in the short- to medium-term, yet spending a little time to plan the day or the week ahead can make a big difference to how healthy our lifestyle is, both physically and mentally. One of the most fundamental changes we can make to improve our well-being is to our diet; making a record of what you consume over a few days can be a real eye-opener and balancing your diet should be a priority. The changes may feel strange at first, but the benefits to your life should soon become apparent and the alterations will soon cease to seem like sacrifices.

The amount of exercise that people undertake in the developed world is far below what is considered a healthy level for an adult, yet it is surprising how easy it can be to incorporate an effective amount into your daily routine. As well as exercises that you can perform in the morning or early evening, most people will find it easy to incorporate more walking in their working day, for example.

With work being one of the most common causes of stress in our lives, it is not surprising that it is also one of the most fruitful areas for change, from the moment your alarm goes off in the morning to the time you return home in the evening. Paradoxically, planning short breaks at work and knowing how to switch off at the end of the day can lead to a more productive day in the long term. And if our homes are where we go to relax, it is sensible to make them as tranquil as possible, especially if you spend time at home during the day.

Our daily lives and the world around us may seem full of sources of stress, yet with planning, thought and a positive outlook we can make every aspect and every situation a source of peace, pleasure and tranquillity.

Try not to be a slave to a schedule – take the opportunity to slow down and enjoy the many things each day has to offer.

Change your lifestyle and do 10 minutes of stretching, yoga or Pilates each morning – it will improve your health and fitness and give you more energy for the coming day.

Diet

'You are what you eat' is one of those irritating platitudes that happens to be true. Stuff yourself with junk food or drink too much alcohol and you will feel tired, bloated and sluggish. Eat a well-balanced diet with plenty of fresh fruit and vegetables and you will feel much more alert and full of increased vitality and vigour.

A balanced diet

Eating the right balance of food can make a big difference to your health and vitality. Your body needs a diet that consists of about 50% carbohydrates, 30% fat, 15% protein and plenty of fibre, vitamins and minerals and water.

Carbohydrates

These provide the body's basic source of energy. Simple carbohydrates, such as sugars, give instant energy but have no nutritional value. Complex carbohydrates, found in bread, pasta, rice, potatoes, cereals and pulses, are better for you because they are slow-releasing.

The foods that contain complex carbohydrates also contain fibre, minerals and essential vitamins.

Fats

These are essential for growth and healthy digestion, but too much fat can make you overweight and cause serious health problems.

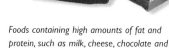

Foods containing high amounts of fat and protein, such as milk, cheese, chocolate and bacon, are best eaten in small quantities.

Protein

The body needs a daily supply of protein for cell growth, maintenance and repair. Most Westerners get much more protein than they need, which usually becomes converted into fat.

Pulses, rice and nuts are high in fibre, carbohydrate and protein, and provide essential bulk for the diet.

Fibre

Dietary fibre, found in nuts, pulses, rice, cereals and wholegrains, prevents constipation, lowers blood cholesterol and helps protect against bowel disorders and diseases.

Vitamins and minerals

Although only needed in small amounts, these are essential for maintaining good health.

Foods for relaxation

Foods that contain calcium, magnesium and vitamin B6 are known to have a tranquilizing effect. Green leafy vegetables, milk and dairy products, apricots, bananas, nuts and yeast extract are just some of the foods that will help you feel calmer. Meat, milk and eggs contain tryptophan, an essential amino acid that turns into the important brain chemical serotonin, which enhances mood and regulates sleep.

What to eat

The healthiest diet is one that is high in fruit, vegetables, grains and pulses and low in animal and dairy products. Nutritional guidelines are based on the traditional eating habits of people who live around the Mediterranean, where there is a history of long life expectancy and low rates of heart disease.

- Complex carbohydrates should form half your daily diet.
- Eat at least five portions of fruit and vegetables a day, preferably organic.
- Try to consume low-fat dairy foods.
- Eat oily fish at least once a week.
- Limit your consumption of red meat and cheeses.
- Eat plenty of fibre-rich foods.
- Reduce your salt intake – use in cooking only.
- Limit your sugar intake – try not to use too much in tea and coffee.
- Eat fresh foods whenever possible and cut back on processed foods.
- Drink alcohol in moderation, and try to have at least two alcohol-free days a week.
- Drink enough fluids to keep your urine pale – at least two litres of water a day to flush out toxins. A glass of water every couple of hours will make you feel much more alert.
- Limit your consumption of tea, coffee, cola-type drinks and chocolate.

When to eat

Optimum nutrition means eating the right foods at the right time, and good health depends on eating regular meals. Breakfast kick-starts the metabolism and boosts blood-sugar levels: if you miss it you may feel tired and unable to concentrate. Lunch should be the biggest meal of the day because this is when the metabolism is at its most effective. Have a light supper at least two hours before you go to bed as it is hard for the body to digest a large meal at the end of the day.

How to eat

A leisurely meal is much more enjoyable than a snack on the hoof, and infinitely more relaxing. The next time you eat, sit down and savour each mouthful. Experience the different flavours and notice how they complement each other. If you are drinking a glass of wine, wait before swallowing and allow the complexities of taste to become apparent. As you chew, appreciate the different textures of food. If you take time to appreciate food you are less likely to overeat and more likely to chew properly, which will benefit your digestion.

The problem with stimulants

Stimulants, such as tea, coffee, chocolate and sugar, are chemicals that act on the body like rocket fuel, giving a quick burst of energy followed by a rapid burnout. They boost your energy levels by stimulating the adrenal glands, which sit on top of the kidneys and release hormones that give your body's cells an express delivery of glucose. You soon become caught in a vicious circle whereby you need more of the stimulant to get the same effect until you become dependent upon it. Stimulants also contain toxins, and your body has only a finite capacity to deal with these. As your body's chemistry becomes more exhausted, your body is in a constant state of red alert and you become prey to anxiety, fatigue, and mood swings.

After eight o'clock at night you should have no more than a light meal to ensure effective digestion.

Reducing dependencies on stimulants, such as coffee, tea, chocolate and sugar will make you feel much calmer and healthier.

Reducing stimulant dependence

Cutting down on stimulants is essential to helping you feel relaxed. Keep a diary for three days to identify which stimulants you rely on and be honest about just how much of each you are consuming. Try to identify at which point in the day you usually take them (as a reaction to a stressful situation, or as a pick-me-up, for example) and see if a pattern emerges. Try to replace these behaviour patterns with healthier ones, such as eating a piece of fruit instead of a bar of chocolate.

Cutting out stimulants completely is impossible for most people, but the way to cut down is to target one at a time and reduce your intake until it is no longer a daily necessity. You will probably feel groggy and get regular headaches for the first few days (particularly if you are addicted to coffee), but persevere and you will soon feel much better and healthier.

Nicotine and alcohol dependence are very hard habits to overcome, and may require professional counselling or group therapy.

Bowl of fruit

Buy a large fruit bowl and keep it well stocked with plenty of fresh, appetising fruit, such as bananas, apples and oranges. Next time you want a snack, avoid the biscuit tin and head for the fruit bowl instead.

The importance of exercise

One of the first things we neglect to do when stressed is to exercise. However, research has proven that exercise is a tremendous relaxation aid. Regular exercise frees your mind and your body: it can improve mood, increase self-esteem, reduce anxiety, promote sleep, reduce high blood pressure, and help weight loss.

How exercise helps you relax

1. Exercise stimulates the appetite. Those who exercise regularly tend to eat better, and good nutrition helps your body to manage stress more effectively.

2. Exercise causes the release of the body's natural painkillers, endorphins, which reduce anxiety and leave you feeling relaxed and in a better mood.

3. Exercise releases adrenaline, which builds up in your body when you are stressed.

4. Muscular movement enables the body's systems to work more efficiently, removing toxins.

5. Physical activity makes you feel more confident about your body.

6. Exercise forces you to make time for yourself, distracting you from daily pressures, which will in turn reduce stress. Repetitive exercise such as walking, running or swimming is a golden opportunity for reflection, meditation and mental relaxation.

7. Regular exercise will make you tired and help you sleep better (although strenuous exercise just before bedtime can stimulate the body too much).

8. Exercise promotes deep breathing, which is key to relaxation. And deep breathing will supply more oxygen to the brain, which improves mental stamina.

Practising yoga is a great way of improving your physical health and reducing stress into the bargain.

Getting started

It is important to choose an activity you enjoy, because you are then much more likely to stick to it. Find an activity that suits your personality, and think of exercise as a joy and a means of relaxation rather than a chore. If you can keep to a regular programme for at least six months, the chances are that you will continue for much longer. Consider your physical limitations and don't push your body too severely. Build up gradually, especially if you have not exercised for a while.

Improving general fitness

You don't have to give a lot of time, or join a gym or spend lots of money to become fit. As little as 10 minutes a day of walking, dancing, gardening, swimming or cycling can make a significant difference to your overall fitness levels, dramatically reduce stress and make you feel more energetic, healthier and happier.

You can choose forms of exercise that are easily incorporated into your daily life: walk or cycle to work if you can; walk up the stairs instead of taking the lift; get off the bus to work one or two stops earlier and walk the remaining distance; regularly take the dog for a walk; take the children to the park at the weekend; or just put on some music and dance around the kitchen.

Caution

Consult a doctor before embarking on a vigorous programme of exercise if your lifestyle is very sedentary, if you are pregnant, if you are over 45 years of age, if you have a history of high blood pressure, high cholesterol levels, heart or lung disease, or if you are a heavy smoker or considerably overweight.

Cycling is a great way to get plenty of fresh air and improve your cardiovascular fitness.

World of work

Most of us spend the majority of our day at work, and research shows that the hours we spend working are constantly increasing. You are unlikely to be able to change either the prevailing work ethic or your working environment, but you can keep hold of your priorities and devise strict routines to ensure you make the most of your time.

How to organise your day

If you're one of those people who, having rushed out of the door in the morning, has to return because you have forgotten something, or if you are someone who spends much of your working day flapping about until you reach home in a state of exhaustion, you need to get organised and regain control.

Try out the following advice to take control of your day and reduce stress:

- Prepare as much as possible the night before – put your clothes out, or lay the breakfast table, for example.

- Get up at least 10 minutes earlier than usual to give yourself the extra time to complete whatever it is that causes you to rush.

- Do not switch on the television as this will distract you and make you late.

- Do not answer the phone unless you think it could be really important.

- Just before leaving the house, go over your mental checklist to reassure yourself you have everything you need.

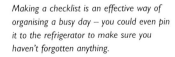

Making a checklist is an effective way of organising a busy day – you could even pin it to the refrigerator to make sure you haven't forgotten anything.

At work

Having a work routine helps you define your achievements and leave the stresses of work behind at the end of the day. Once a week, plan a weekly schedule. Then spend the first 15 minutes of each working day thinking about what you wish to achieve. It helps to make a list, but don't make it too long as this can be daunting and demotivating.

- Don't try to do too many things at once.

- Prioritise, and do the essential things first.

- Try to tackle at least one thing on your list that you really do not like doing – you will have a great sense of achievement when this task is completed.

- Leave half an hour a day for the unexpected.

- Delegate as many tasks as possible – don't take on everything yourself.

- If you can't delegate, ask for help.

- Learn to say 'no' politely, without feeling the need to justify yourself.

- Get a good diary and use it.

- Meetings should be to the point – always make it clear when it will end.

- If you are delayed, phone and inform the person you are meeting; if you have to break an appointment, try to give as much notice as possible.

- Take time at the end of the day to review what you've done and to congratulate yourself on your achievements.

Telephone taming

- If you have to make a number of phone calls, group them together – it is much more efficient.

- Use an answering machine and switch off your mobile phone if you do not wish to be disturbed.

- If you work from home, invest in an extra line and don't answer the business one out of office hours.

- Do not answer the phone just before or during meals – if it is really important, the person will phone back.

Don't let the telephone take over your life – only answer calls when it suits you, and only make calls when you have plenty of time.

Work space

A cluttered desk makes it more difficult to work effectively. Tidy your desk at the end of each day. Make use of in, out and pending trays, and keep everything you need close to hand. Keep a supply of stationery and pens within easy reach of your desk, and dispose of those that no longer work.

Pause for thought

Most of us are governed by clocks, constantly under one deadline or another in order to become more efficient and productive. As slaves of time, we constantly rush to get things done, frequently making mistakes, instead of thinking about what we are trying to achieve. Taking a moment to stop and think gives you the opportunity to act with greater consciousness and react more appropriately to the situation. A pause also lets you say 'no' and avoid committing yourself to too many things at once.

At work, take time to enjoy a tasty, nutritious snack and recharge your batteries.

Take a break

It is universally recognised that to work for long hours without a regular break is damaging for your health and can on occasion be extremely dangerous. It's just like driving – you have to stop every couple of hours as your concentration and abilities begin to fail. Many office chairs are bad for the posture, and long hours spent staring at a computer screen can cause eyestrain, neck ache and backache. Get up, stretch, and walk around at least once an hour. Take time off for lunch and eat away from your desk if possible. Remember that by law you are entitled to have regular breaks, and you will be much more productive if you take them.

When to switch off

Don't fall into the trap of thinking that the longer you spend at work, the more you will get done when in fact the opposite is more likely. Working excessively long hours and taking work home is counterproductive. Keeping work and home separate, and being able to spend quality time with your family, is essential – if you spend your leisure time relaxing, you will return to work refreshed and be able to give it your full attention.

Instant calm at work

If you are being thrown into a state of panic by an approaching deadline, make a conscious effort to calm down. Instruct yourself to stop, then close your eyes and breathe slowly and deeply. Feel yourself becoming more relaxed; notice your heartbeat slowing down. Alternatively, follow the steps for quick and easy meditation on page 25.

Time off: holidays

A holiday is a chance to rest and recharge your batteries, but all too often it turns into another stressful event. Mental and physical preparation will make potential difficulties easier to deal with. Planning is key to a successful holiday. First of all, choose a holiday that suits you and your family. Find out as much as you can about your destination before you go so that you know what your itinerary will be, and what to pack. A few days before, prepare yourself mentally by making an effort to relax and slow down – maybe take an extra day off work to unwind further.

Relaxing at home

Your home is your sanctuary. Your living environment has a tremendous impact on your sense of well-being. An untidy, cluttered home painted in dingy colours makes you feel stressed, while a bright, tidy home that reflects your character and family will create a happy, positive and loving atmosphere where you can truly relax.

Light and space

Natural light is best for your eyes, so make the most of daylight and position desks near windows. A spacious, airy and light environment is the most relaxing, but you can create space by keeping surfaces clear.

Turn down the volume

Noise can be incredibly stressful, even though you may not be aware of it. Only watch television if there's a programme you really want to see, and turn it off at mealtimes. Soothe your soul by listening to music instead.

To create a serene atmosphere in your home, avoid harsh fluorescent lighting, and use soft light or candles in the evening.

Ten top tips for a tidy home

1. Remove your shoes at the door — it stops you bringing dirt into the house.

2. Do your least favourite household chore first.

3. Keep a waste-paper bin in each room.

4. The less you have, the easier it is to keep clean. Clear away clutter once a month and have a good sort out once a year. If you haven't used something in the last year, then you probably don't need it.

5. Keep work surfaces tidy.

6. Storage space is essential — invest in extra cupboards if you need them.

7. Encourage your children to tidy up after themselves.

8. To discourage random clutter, keep a 'lost property box' in the living room.

9. Tidy up after a meal rather than leaving the dishes until morning.

10. Organise a rota so that each family member plays their part.

*Encourage your children
to help keep the house
clean and tidy.*

Feng shui

Feng shui is the ancient Chinese art of arranging living and working spaces so that they are in harmony with the flow of *qi*, the universal life force (see page 19). Landscapes, buildings and rooms are said to have their own flow of *qi*, and feng shui encourages blocked or diminished *qi* to move more freely in a certain area by altering its layout. A feng shui practitioner will make a detailed assessment of each room in your house and suggest changes, such as a new colour scheme or repositioning of plants and furniture.

To improve the feng shui in your home, clear up clutter and make sure there is plenty of space around furniture.

The world around you

Those who appreciate nature are generally happier, calmer people. Today, many people live in noisy, polluted, overcrowded cities where concrete predominates over greenery. But you don't have to live in the country to benefit from nature. Take a walk through the park or simply sit in the garden to relax and truly appreciate your surroundings.

The great outdoors

Ultimately, a relaxed state of being depends on you spending plenty of time outdoors. Light is recognised as essential for regulating the body's internal clock, which controls hormone production and sleep. Spend holidays in the mountains or at the seaside to get maximum benefit from light and fresh air.

Plants pour oxygen into the environment while soaking up carbon dioxide and other toxins.

Park life

A walk in the park will help you to reconnect with the natural world. Visit the same park during each of the seasons so that you can appreciate nature's life cycle. Take time to notice the colours of the trees and flowers and the different smells. Breathe in deeply and inhale large amounts of fresh air.

Gardening

Gardening is a wonderfully relaxing activity because it releases physical tension, thus reducing the amount of circulating stress hormones in the body, while the act of cultivation in itself is soothing for the soul. Novice gardeners can nurture hardy, low-maintenance plants (see gardening books for inspiration and practical advice). If you don't have a garden, plant a window box instead.

Improve the oxygen levels in your home by keeping some pot plants.

Seasons

Air conditioning and modern central heating systems have removed much of the impact of the changing seasons, but if you can live in harmony with nature's cycle you will appreciate life much more. Spring, traditionally the season of hope and renewal, is the time for starting afresh, clearing your life of clutter and setting change in motion. Summer, associated with happiness and light, brings a sense of freedom and carefreeness. Autumn, the season of fruition and abundance, is the time for reflecting upon what you have achieved and counting the year's blessings. Winter is a time of rest, retreat and reflection on what has passed.

Never judge a day by the weather

All too often we let the weather determine our mood: on a sunny day, a good mood; on a rainy day, gloom and introspection. Think positively about the different aspects of weather instead: the cool, crispness of snow, the rain that nurtures crops or the fact that thunderstorms do literally clear the air.

A sense of time

Your body adheres to a natural sense of time without you even being aware of it. Ask yourself how often you really need to know what the time is.

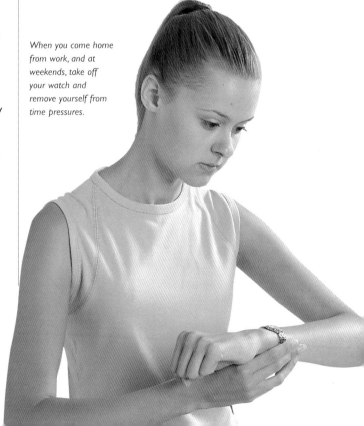

When you come home from work, and at weekends, take off your watch and remove yourself from time pressures.

Getting a good night's sleep

A good night's sleep is a period of profound rest that is essential for your physical and emotional well-being. Time spent sleeping is often the best way to recover from illness or cope with stress. When sleeping, your body will repair and regenerate itself, and your mind can resolve outstanding problems through dreams.

What is sleep?

Sleep is a naturally occurring state of unconsciousness, when the electrical activity of the brain is more rhythmical than when awake and reacts less to outside stimuli. There are two basic sleep states: deep sleep, known as non-REM (NREM) sleep, when the body repairs itself, interrupted by episodes of Rapid Eye Movement (REM) sleep, when most dreaming takes place.

Establishing a calming routine that helps you wind down and relax before bedtime will go a long way in helping you to get a good night's sleep.

How much sleep?

The amount of sleep necessary to be fully rested varies for each individual, and it decreases with age. Most adults get by on seven to eight hours sleep, though some sleep experts claim we need more. The elderly can function on five or six hours a night.

Sleep problems

Sleep is one of the first things to suffer when you are stressed, and too little sleep will make you tired and irritable. A lack of sleep is itself a stress factor, and it is all too easy to become locked into a cycle of sleeplessness that is difficult to break. There are many different kinds of sleeplessness, including not being able to go to sleep, frequent waking, and waking too early in the morning.

Sleep enhancers

- Don't go to bed hungry, but avoid large meals before bedtime.

- Bananas, milky drinks and wholemeal biscuits are calming foods and ideal for eating before you go to sleep.

- Caffeine, alcohol and nicotine all disturb sleep. Drink a cup of warm herbal tea before bedtime – chamomile is particularly effective.

- Exercise during the day will remove stress hormones from your body but avoid any form of exercise (apart from sex) at least three hours before bedtime.

Drink something calming and tasty before you sleep.

Establishing a routine

- Stop work at least an hour before bedtime to calm mental activity.

- A warm bath before bedtime will relax your muscles and soothe your body.

- Go to bed at the same time each night and get up at a regular time.

- Your bedroom needs to be a place for sleeping rather than an extension of your office or living room – keep it quiet and warm.

- If you really cannot sleep, get up and go into another room and read a book or watch something light on television until you feel sleepy.

The importance of dreams

We all have dreams, although we may not remember them when we wake up. Dreaming is thought to act as a psychological safety valve, allowing us to work through problems, emotions and anxieties so we can start afresh each day.

Natural remedies for relaxation

Natural remedies are very effective in reducing the effects of stress and restoring the balance of body and mind. They are an enjoyable way of improving well-being and have been used around the world for thousands of years.

Aromatherapy

Essential oils distilled from plants, flowers and resins can be used to promote good health and help you relax. Your sense of smell is directly linked to memories and mood (see page 29). Among other things, essential oils can be antidepressant, relieve pain and tension, ease headaches, act as a tonic, and help to ensure a good night's sleep.

There are few things more relaxing than an aromatherapy massage – the treatment eases muscular tension while treating the senses to the soothing aroma of essential oils.

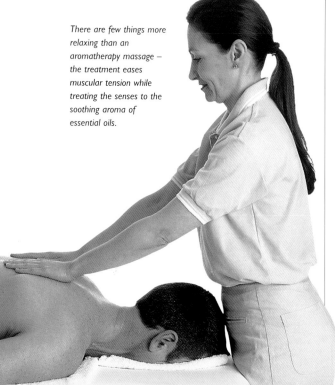

Oils can be inhaled, used in compresses to relieve pain, added to bathwater or massage oil, or used in a vaporiser.

Massage

An aromatherapy massage combines the relaxing properties of various oils with the benefits of touch. Dilute a few drops of two or three essential oils in a carrier oil such as sweet almond or apricot kernel oil; add a little jojoba oil for very dry skins. Blend six drops of essential oil with 4 tsp (15–20ml) of carrier oil to make enough for a full body massage.

Baths

Only add neat oils to bathwater if they are guaranteed to be non-irritants, such as Roman chamomile and lavender; otherwise, dilute in a carrier oil. Add five drops then swirl the bathwater around to disperse the oils before stepping into the bath. Oils added to bathwater are inhaled and partly absorbed by the skin, bringing immediate physical benefits.

Ten relaxing essential oils

Bergamot (*Citrus bergamia*): soothing, uplifting and good for tension and depression.

Chamomile (*Chamaemelum nobile*): calming; suitable for insomnia.

Jasmine (*Jasminum officinale*): a stimulant or a sedative, according to need; excellent antidepressant and aphrodisiac.

Juniper (*Juniperus communis*): good for fatigue and boosting self-esteem.

Lavender (*Lavandula angustifolia*): a very useful and popular oil, used for relaxing and as an antidepressant and painkiller.

Lemon balm (*Melissa officinalis*): long used to banish melancholy; balances the emotions.

Rosemary (*Rosmarinus officinalis*): refreshing and stimulating.

Sandalwood (*Santalum album*): used as an antidepressant and aphrodisiac.

Vetiver (*Vetiveria zizanioides*): balances the nervous system; good for insomnia.

Ylang ylang (*Cananga odorata*): calming; used as an aphrodisiac and good for panic attacks.

Cautions

* Always dilute oils before use (although lavender and tea tree can be used neat in first aid situations).

* Some oils are not safe to use in pregnancy.

* Seek professional advice before using essential oils if you have a long-standing medical condition such as heart disease, diabetes or high blood pressure.

* Many oils are not suitable for small children, so check first.

* Some oils react adversely to sunlight.

* Do not use steam inhalations if you have a breathing disorder such as asthma.

* Never take oils internally, unless professionally prescribed.

Vaporisation

Filling a room with an aroma of your choice is the easiest way to enjoy essential oils. Add a few drops to a saucer of water and place on a radiator, or place in a burner.

Certain oils can improve mood and concentration, and are deeply relaxing.

Herbalism

Herbal remedies use plants to restore health and strengthen the body, enabling it to recover more easily. Many synthetic drugs, such as aspirin, are derived from plants, but herbalism uses the whole plant, believing that the complex mix of components creates a herbal 'synergy' that is more effective than isolated constituents.

Using herbal remedies

Herbs are usually taken in the form of infusions, tinctures and decoctions. They can also be made into ointments, massage oils and creams to rub into the skin, and added to hot or cold compresses. Many preparations can be bought ready-made from health stores.

Decoctions

Tough plant material such as roots and bark are boiled in water to extract the active ingredients. The liquid is then strained and taken hot or cold. Boil down the liquid and add sugar to make a syrup.

Infusions

An infusion is a herbal tea. Herbs are placed in a teapot, covered with boiling water and left to steam for about 10 minutes. The liquid is drained into a cup and drunk hot or cold. It can be kept in the refrigerator for 24 hours and can be reheated.

Tinctures

Tinctures are made by steeping herbs in a mixture of alcohol and water. The alcohol acts as a preservative (the mixture can be kept for up to two years) and also extracts the medicinal constituents of the plant.

Caution

- Seek professional advice before taking herbal medicine if you are pregnant, or if you have a long-standing medical condition such as heart disease, diabetes or high blood pressure.

- Consult a qualified herbalist before using herbal remedies if you are taking prescribed medication.

Herbal remedies are a natural way of easing away the stresses of modern living. Remember not to exceed the recommended dose.

Popular herbs for relaxation

Chamomile (*Chamaemelum nobile*): promotes feelings of relaxation and settles digestion.

Echinacea (*Echinacea purpurea*): strengthens the immune system.

Ginkgo (*Ginkgo biloba*): improves blood flow and the activity of neurotransmitters in the brain; beneficial for sufferers of tinnitus.

Lavender (*Lavandula angustifolia*): lifts mood and relieves indigestion and headaches.

Lime flower (*Tilia cordata*): effective relaxant that reduces anxiety and restlessness.

St John's wort (*Hypericum perforatum*): a well-known antidepressant without side-effects.

Skullcap (*Scutellaria lateriflora*): a calming nerve tonic that reduces anxiety and restlessness.

Vervain (*Verbena officinalis*): sedative nerve tonic good for insomnia and for relieving tension and depression.

Flower remedies

Flower essences, made by infusing flower heads in water then preserving the strained water in brandy, were developed in the 1920s by an English doctor and homeopath, Edward Bach. He believed that flowers possessed healing properties that could treat emotional illnesses. He thought that harmful emotions were the main cause of disease and identified seven states of mind – fear, uncertainty, lack of interest in present circumstances, loneliness, over-sensitivity, despondency and over-concern for the welfare of others – which he subdivided into 38 negative feelings, each associated with a particular plant. Bach flower remedies aim to restore the harmony of mind and body necessary for good health. That flower remedies work is indisputable, although no one knows how: they do not work in any biochemical way, but therapists believe the remedies contain the energy, or imprint, of the plant and provide a stimulus to kick-start your own healing mechanism.

Glossary

Adrenaline
This is the hormone secreted by the adrenal glands that prepares the body for 'fight or flight' and has widespread effects on circulation, the muscles and the metabolic rate.

Amino acids
These are organic compounds found in proteins. Essential amino acids cannot be made by the body and must be obtained from food.

Autonomic nervous system
The part of the nervous system responsible for automatic body functions, such as breathing, perspiration, salivation, digestion and heart rate. The sympathetic division activates the body's alarm response and prepares for action; the parasympathetic division is concerned with restoring and conserving bodily resources.

Cardiovascular system
The heart and blood vessels.

Central nervous system
The vast network of cells that carry information in the form of electrical impulses to and from all parts of the body to cause bodily activity.

Cholesterol
A fat-like substance present in the blood and most tissues; high levels can damage blood vessel walls and lead to a thickening of the arteries. Excessively high levels of cholesterol can lead to heart problems.

Endorphin
A painkiller produced by the body.

Hormone
A substance produced in one part of the body that travels in the bloodstream to another organ or tissue, where it acts to modify structure or functions.

Hyperventilation
This is breathing at an abnormally rapid rate, which can lead to loss of consciousness as blood acidity falls dramatically.

Immune system
These are the organs responsible for immunity with the ability to resist infection.

Metabolism
Chemical processes that take place in the body, which enable continued growth and functioning of the whole system.

Neurotransmitter
A chemical that is released from nerve endings to transmit impulses between nerves, muscles and glands.

Proteins
Essential constituents of the body that form its structural material and, as enzymes and hormones, regulate body functions.

Qi
The universal 'life force' of traditional Chinese medicine (also known as *chi*); similar to *prana* in Ayurvedic medicine.

Serotonin
A neurotransmitter whose levels in the brain have an important effect on mood.

Stimulant
Something that has an uplifting effect on the mind or body. Well-known stimulants include nicotine, alcohol, sugar, coffee, tea and chocolate.

Useful addresses

Autogenic Training

British Association for Autogenic
Training and Therapy
c/o The Royal London Homeopathic
Hospital NHS Trust
Great Ormond Street
London WC1N 3HR

Alexander Technique

The Society of Teachers of the Alexander Technique
20 London House
266 Fulham Road
London SW10 9EL

Aromatherapy

Aromatherapy Organisations Council
3 Latymer Close
Braybooke
Market Harborough
Leics LE16 8LN

Herbalism

National Institute of Medical Herbalists
56 Longbrook Street
Exeter
Devon EX4 6AG

Hypnotherapy

The Central Register of Advanced Hypnotherapists
28 Finsbury Park Road
London N4 2JX

Massage

British Massage Therapy Council
Greenbank House
65a Adelphi Street
Preston
Lancs PR1 7BH

Meditation

School of Meditation
158 Holland Park Road
London W11 4UH

Nutrition

The Institute for Optimum Nutrition
Blades Court
Deodar Road
London SW15 2NU

Reflexology

British Reflexology Association
Monks Orchard
Whitbourne
Worcester WR6 5RB

Relaxation and Breathing

The Relaxation for Living Trust
Foxhills
30 Victoria Avenue
Shanklin
Isle of Wight PO37 6LS

T'ai Chi

T'ai Chi Union for Great Britain
23 Oakwood Avenue
Mitcham
Surrey CR4 3DQ

Yoga

British Wheel of Yoga
1 Hamilton Place
Sleaford
Notts NG34 7ES

Visualisation

United Kingdom Council for Psychotherapy
167–69 Great Portland Street
London W1N 5FB

Index